# BORO MAKING FOR BEGINNERS

The Ultimate Picture Guide on How to Make Traditional Japanese Boro from Scratch Including Japanese Boro Stitching Designs and Patterns

Boris Joseph
Copyright@2~~

D1533216

1

# TABLE OF CONTENT

# CHAPTER 1

## INTRODUCTION

It's fashioned out of old t-shirts and it's rather intriguing to look at. I want to point out, however, that despite the fact that this project was a wonderful first try, it was not a complete and utter failure on my part in terms of final success. The problem is that I'm not a particularly talented sewer and have just a limited amount of experience creating items of this nature. Aside from that, it was one of those undertakings that rarely turned out well the first time around. Some things didn't function as planned, and it's a little shabby in some areas... but I've addressed those parts in the guide so that you don't have to make the same mistakes I did. Also, with that said, there's nothing wrong with the overall concept or the main premise, so it may come out lot better in more experienced hands than it did with mine, and I encourage giving it a shot nonetheless.

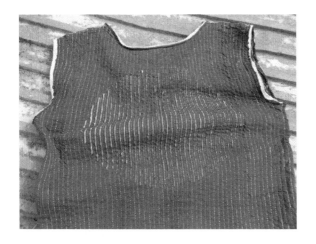

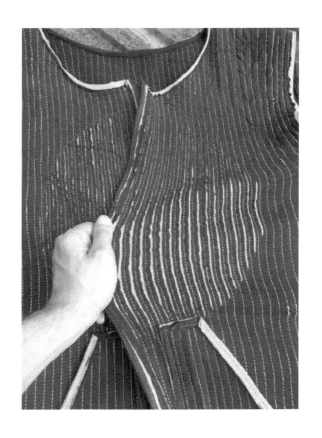

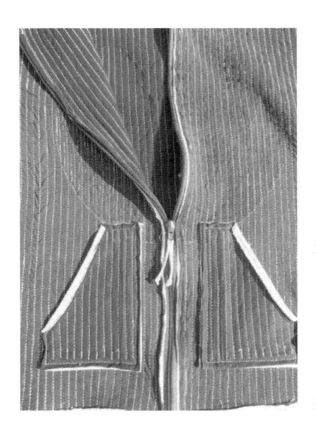

7

# CHAPTER 2

## STEP BY STEP TO MAKE JAPANESE BORO

As a result of my elder brother's generosity, I've been given a large number of t-shirts to wear. Step 1: The t-shirts are one size larger than my usual size, and I already have enough of t-shirts of my own to wear, so I really didn't have a purpose for them... That is, until I come up with an idea.

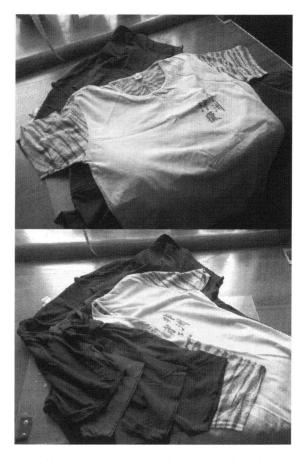

You'll need a couple t-shirts for this craft, so gather your supplies. Perhaps some of your old ones, or you might get some from the second hand shop. In fact, it is OK if they have a few little holes in them. If you want a thicker and warmer vest, even 7 is a good amount to use. For my vest, I used 4 (although I did not use the blue one in the photo).

With one shirt in a contrasting color, you can include some interesting ornamental aspects into your design, as I did, but there is a lot of room for creative experimentation, so you may try something else in terms of color or, on the other hand, keep it very basic.

Also required are an ample supply of thread and a sewing machine, in addition to a variety of other standard equipment and materials.. And if you're

11

excellent at handstitching and don't mind doing a lot of it, you can complete this project without the use of a sewing machine; however, the technique will be slightly different for you starting at a certain point in the lesson.

Step 2: However, before moving on, I'd want to say a few words about the project's origins and motivation.

13

It is known as boro in Japan for a traditional method of repairing clothing that entails stitching patches of fabric onto garments with many stitches, a technique that has been around for centuries (mainly in parallel lines). Fabric was quite expensive in the olden days, therefore even the wealthiest of individuals would repair their kimonos in this manner. Throughout time, layers of patches accumulated, making the material thicker and, as a result, more appropriate for wearing in colder weather.

On the photographs of boro textiles, it can be seen that the cloth on the highpoints is frequently rubbed through, revealing underlaying layers of fabric of varying colors underneath the surface cloth. This has the inadvertent effect of creating an intriguing ornamental look.

The practical side of things like this fascinates me, and the general aesthetics of boro textiles appeal to me, so with my project, I'm attempting to mimic both, but in a more stylized fashion rather than in a strictly literal one.

Step 3: All right, let's get started.

The t-shirt-shaped frame, into which the shirts will be dragged for more convenient treatment in subsequent phases, is a critical component of the entire project. I created it out of a piece of corrugated cardboard that was rigid.

First, I sketched up a basic outline using some of the shirts I had on hand. After that, I used the ruller to define and expand it. The frame had to be somewhat larger than the t-shirts themselves in order for them to be consistently stretched as they were tugged on, but not excessively, during the process.

Later, sleeve parts were added to the design. It may be necessary for them to be able to flex or bend in order for them to be able to pull the shirts over their shoulders.

Step 4: Once the work is completed, it is time to put the shirts on (ontop of each other ofcourse).

23

You might start by wearing a shirt with a contrasting color to create a vibrant interior lining. If there is an image or pattern design on the inside, you may turn it inside out to make it visible. The contrary is also possible, as is making all of them unique in their hues. As I previously stated, the decision is yours; but, I will explain what I did.

As a result, the first two t-shirts I surveyed for the frame are both black. The third one has a bright yellow color. And the final one is dark once more.

Step 5: Use pins to fasten the borders of the creases and flatten the wrinkles. At the same time, avoid stretching the cloth too much in the vertical direction.

Making use of appropriate tools
and templates, draw the lines on
the stack of shirts as follows:

- a vertical line running across the center of the front (the center line);

vertical line running vertically down the middle of the back (the center line);

- a horizontal line at the bottom of the page;

In frame up, indicate the sleaves on both sides of each shirt by following the imaginary line that runs down the sides of the shirts.

- a curled line across the nape of the neck

Make certain that the ends of
the lines are on the same side
on both the front and rear sides.

Lines along the bottom, at the
sleeve ends, and around the
neck are intended to be trimmed
off at a later point in the sewing
process. Making certain that all
of the layers of fabric will be
shown on the edge when the
cuts are done is important when
locating those lines.

The cut along the center line on
the front will also be made later,
but in a slightly different
manner, and I'll talk about it in
more detail later on.

Step 6: Because the zipper is
going to be sewn into the vest,

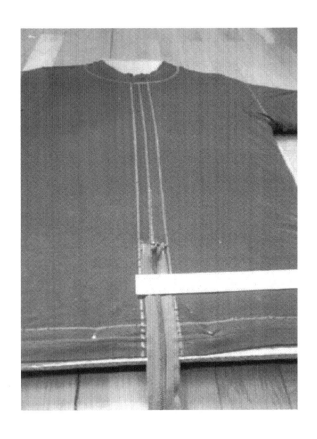

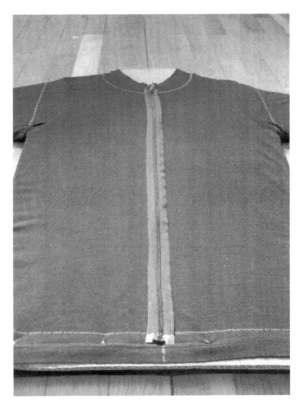

I'm drawing two additional lines that are a little wider than the zipper itself, using the center line on the front as a point of reference.

I'm marking an extra set of lines that are parallel to those that are intended for cutting by walking 1,5-2cm inwards to the body of a t-shirt after the first set of lines that I've already marked. Those will be used for stitching.

In this eighth step, you will learn how to use a comma to separate the words "and" and "and not."

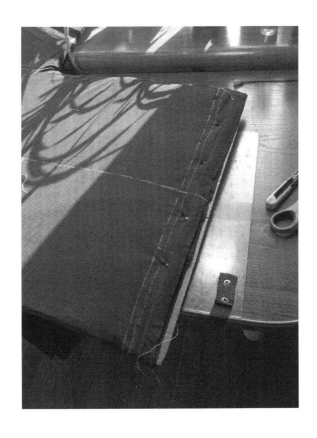

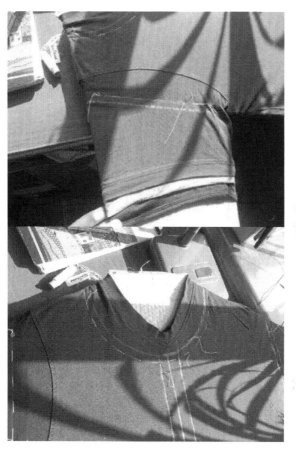

At long last, I'm basting all four layers together via the "sewing" lines (at the bottom, at the sleeve ends, around the neck), through the center line on the back, and through the two "zipper" lines that I indicated earlier.

9. I'm also marking and basting four vertical intermediate lines as part of this step. It will assist in preventing layers from slipping and moving excessively during subsequent procedures.

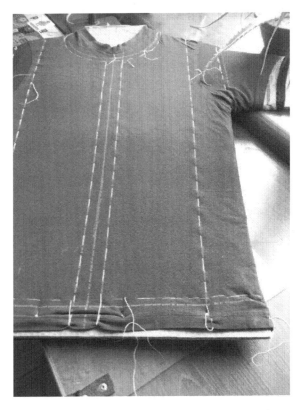

Step 10: It's time to remove the zipper from the bag.

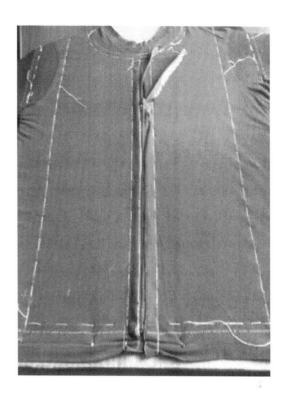

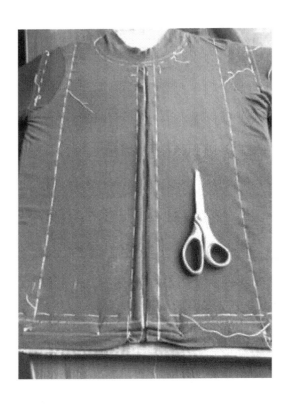

You'll need one of those zip-lock bags that comes apart in two halves when opened.

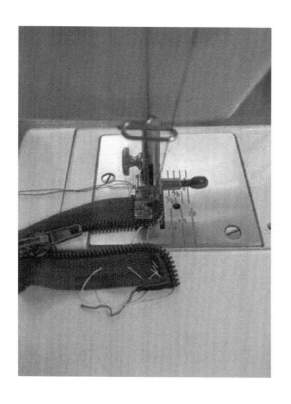

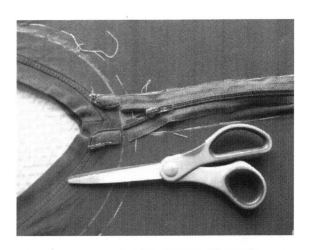

Purchasing a zipper first will allow you to label your t-shirts according to their length, which will save you time in the long run. I discovered mine in my mother's collection of salvaged zippers, and while it was the most appropriate, it was a little too long. If, for whatever reason, this is also your situation, I'll show you what you can do about it in the following step.

Firstly, I'm cutting two top layers of fabric along the center line on the front (which is half of the total amount of layers I have) and setting the zipper in place to measure how long I need the zipper to be.

Then I'm going to add around 2cm to the required length and cut off the extra at the top area of the zipper. Step 12: (where the dog is when it closed). Then I'm going to bend those two petals to the sides and sew them together to make a flower.

Step 12: The zipper now fits perfectly... well, at least in your case, since when you're sewing your vest, you'll already be familiar with the section where I'm talking about the item that didn't function the way I expected it to, and you'll know how to fix it... but that's for later.

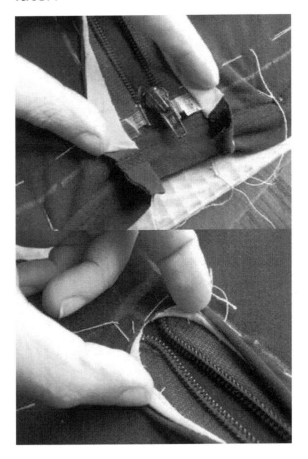

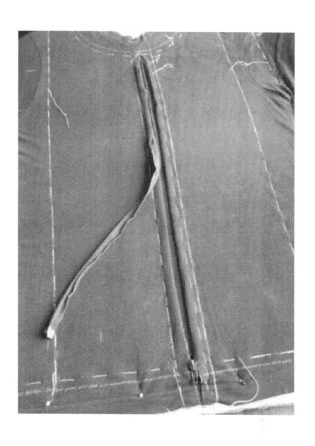

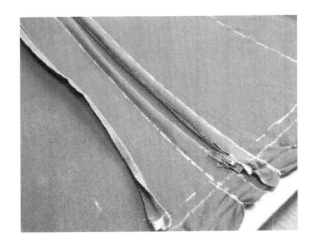

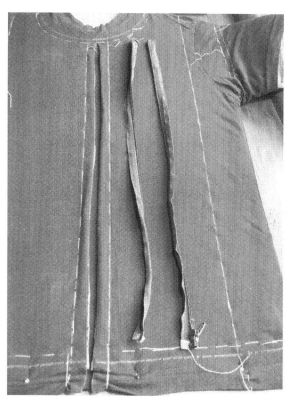

It will be more convenient to utilize the zipper if it is divided into two halves. After that, I'll slip one portion beneath the plap that was made by the cut and secure it in place using basting thread through all four layers. The same may be said for the second section.

Step number thirteen.

61

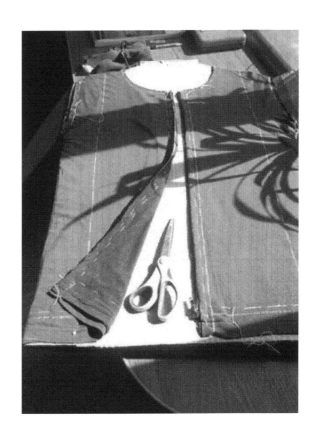

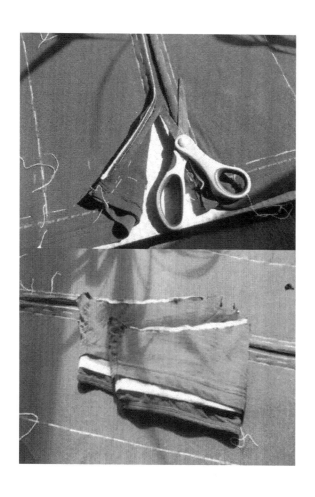

63

This is the point at which our vest may be removed from the frame (or not, if you're hand-sewing it all the way through). But first, it's helpful to cut away some of the "unvanted" sections while the fabric is still in its stretched state. As a result, I'm removing the neck hole as well as the sleaves. Be precise while cutting off sleeve ends since we'll be using them to make pockets and will put them aside after the project is completed.

You may also cut off the bottom section at this point, but I opted to wait a little longer to do so.

At the end, the remaining layers of cloth between the zipper halves were cut away.

Remove the frame from the picture. Please do not throw it out since we will definitely utilize it.

Step 14: It's now time to put the sewing machine to work.

My thread is a bright yellow hue to match the yellow t-shirt I'm stitching on top of.

Put along the basting around the neck and sleeve openings, and then sew the zipper in place at the bottom of the garment.

At this point, I'm going to chop off the bottom of the bottle.

Basting should be removed where it is no longer neaded.

Part of the design that is essential is a pattern of parallel stitches that go over the whole object, giving it a distinct texture while also functionally joining all of the layers of cloth together.

I have to say that sewing all of those seams is a time-consuming procedure, but the end effect is rather distinctive, so it is well worth it.

Use the edge of your sewing machine foot as a guide, and the seam that secures the zipper as a guiding line, to get started sewing your zipper in place. It is more convenient to begin the seam at the bottom and work your way up to the shoulders this way. Make all of your seams go in the same direction and use each new one as a guide line for the one after that. -

Wrinkles on the surface of the skin will almost always appear. Particularly noticeable near the end of the seam. It is created by the foot movement moving and stretching the upper layers of fabric; thus, to minimize the impact, lessen the pressing force of the foot on your sewing machine and raise the foot up and down periodically to release some tension. Another option is to disperse the creases that are still forming as evenly as possible and just stitch them down. In general, such relics are a wonderful compliment to the overall aesthetic. However, it can still seem a little shabby in some spots, like in my case... so there are no guarantees there.

The other aspect of my case that is worth mentioning is the difficulties I had with the thread I used. It was a spool of old cotton thread that I had plucked from a basket of threads that we had on hand. That thing was pathetically weak and kept snipping at me all the time. Consequently, I was unable to properly adjust the thread tension in this situation. It all resulted in a few lost stitches here and there, as well as some overlapped seams where I had to start the seam from the beginning, as you can see in the images. It kind of fit with the overall aesthetics, but it was a complete disaster in terms of functionality. Whatever the case, I had to continue using this thread, at the very least to complete the entire front side of the vest because the new one I purchased was a little thinner and the difference would be inconsequential to the overall look. I had no troubles with the new polyester thread, thus it is true that the thread is key.

Anyhow, continue sewing parallel seams from the zipper to the sides until you reach the end of the row of stitches. Fill both parts of the front with the filling. Remove the basting from the areas where it is no longer neaded.

Step 16: Starting at the center line, stitch your way around the outside of the garment. Then, using it as a guideline, walk away from it and to the sides. As a result, even if there is any unparallelness or irregularity at the point where the rear and front pieces meet, it will appear on the sides, where it is less visible.

Step 17: At this point, it's time to get serious. I was able to tell right away that some things were not going to turn out the way I had hoped they would. I expected that the cut edges would curl up in the same manner that this sort of cloth normally does, displaying brilliant yellow strips of material underneath the cut edges. Because the impact was much more subtle than I had anticipated, I opted to go with a more fake approach to obtain the intended aesthetic. This is most likely what you'll be required to do as well.

As a result, I divided the cloth along the edge into two halves. I stitched it down after folding one portion on top of the other and sewing it to the back. At this point, I realized that I hadn't been as precise as I should have been when cutting since the edges were rather rough in some spots.

In order to make my life a little easier at the zipper, I merely folded the top two layers.

You can see how the zipper is poking out at the bottom now, whereas it was flush with the edge before stitching and folding the edges. This is exactly what I was referring about earlier. While situating the zipper, make any necessary modifications.

After completing Step 18, I had to deal with the pockets, but I was getting a little bored of this job, so I skipped right to the enjoyable part. Step 19:

The peculiar feel of boro textiles, which I discussed previously, was something I wanted to imitate in this project. By cutting through the top black layer of cloth, I hoped to show the contrasting yellow layer beneath it, resulting in a vibrant ornamental effect. However, once again, the end effect was not as vibrant as it had been hoped. Possibly it will become more visually distinctive after a few of washes, or perhaps it is the quality of this specific t-shirt...

In any case, when stretched, it looks extremely nice, so if you find yourself in the Alien movie with a chestburster in your possession, simply put on this vest... it'll look amazing!

As a result, here's what I really did.

First and foremost, I used the plastic lid from the cake package to draw a circle on the chest region of the vest with a piece of dried soap (and this is what I used previously for making all those marks). It may be any shape you choose, as long as it isn't very complicated. Next, using those little scissors with pointed tips, I cut the top layer of cloth between the seams within the region that had been drawn around the fabric.

Step 19: I repeated the process on the back as well.

When stretched, it has a pretty amazing appearance once again.

Step twenty-one

So, it's time to deal with the matter of pockets. This is where we're making use from the sleave cut offs. I'm using only two pairs of them because there's no need for the cloth to be very thick here.

Otherwise there's nothing principaly new here and all the processes are depicted in the photographs.

Step 21:\sA few last touches: cutting off sticking out ends of threads, making that unsightly portion on the shoulders a bit prettier, some embellishments here and there and we're done.

A hood was something I wanted to add, but I didn't have any leftover t-shirts, so I'll probably wait and add it later as an addition to this article.

Step 22: That's all there is to it for now; thank you for your time and consideration, and have a pleasant boro.

**THE END**

Made in United States
Orlando, FL
14 March 2023

31015291R00046